Greenhaven World History Progra[m]

GENERAL EDITORS

Malcolm Yapp
Margaret Killingray
Edmund O'Connor

Cover design by John Castle

ISBN 0-89908-009-X Paper Edition
ISBN 0-89908-034-0 Library Edition

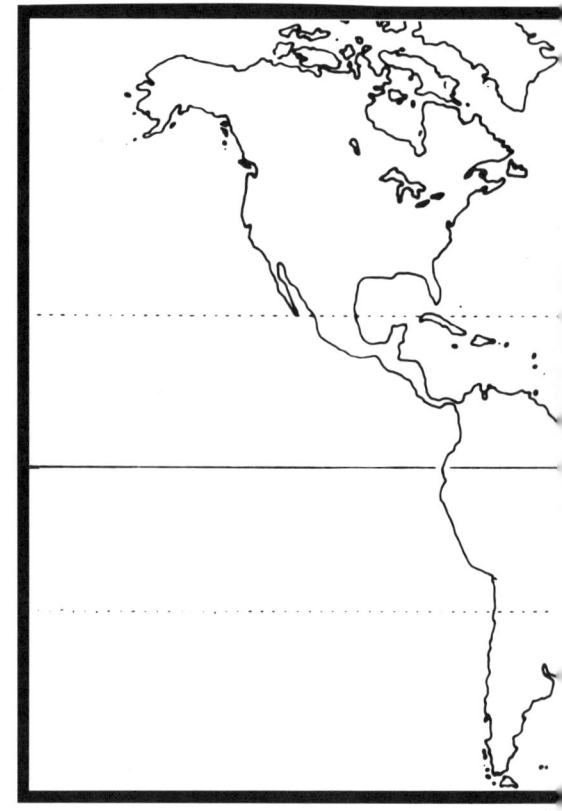

© Copyright 1980 by Greenhaven Press, Inc.

First published in Great Britain 1974 by
GEORGE G. HARRAP & CO. LTD
© George G. Harrap & Co. Ltd 1974

All rights reserved. N[o]
of this publication ma[y]
reproduced in any for[m]
by any means without
prior permission of
Greenhaven Press, Inc

TRADITIONAL AFRICA

by John Addison

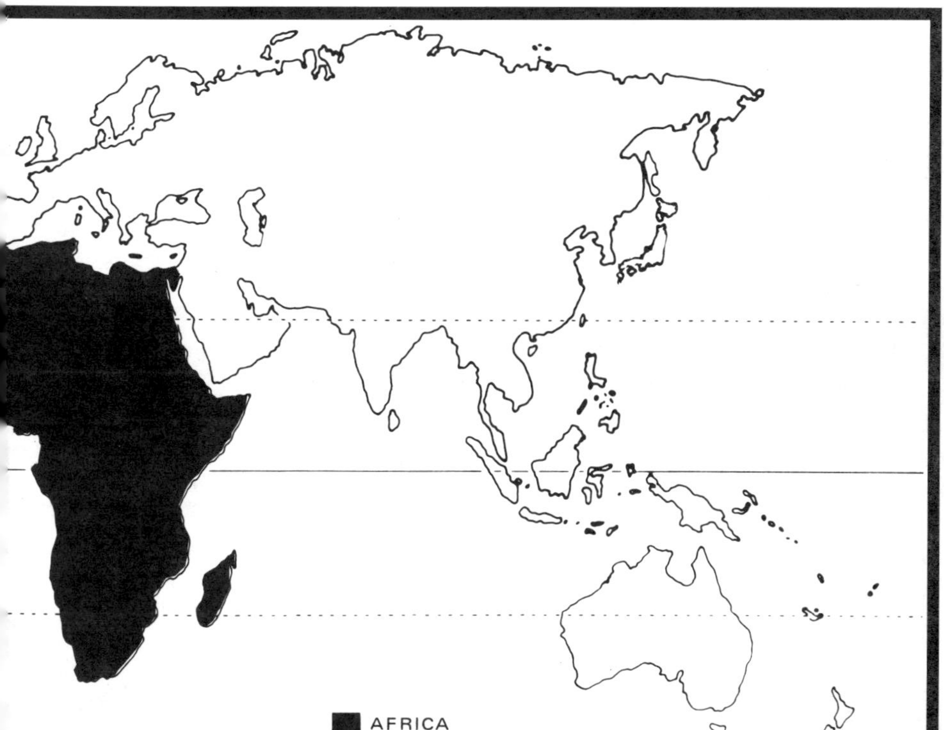

■ AFRICA

Greenhaven Press, Inc.
577 SHOREVIEW PARK ROAD
ST. PAUL, MN 55112

Only forty years ago a leading historian wrote that most Africans 'had no history'. Today hundreds of historians are uncovering and writing the history of Africans from all parts of the continent. The idea that Africa had no important history before the coming of the Europeans was widely believed in the second half of the nineteenth century, when Europeans were busy exploring Africa. At that time western Europe had been experiencing scientific and industrial changes for three centuries. Africa had remained untouched by these changes. Europeans judged Africa by European standards. They took it for granted that their own way of life was 'civilized': that the Africans' way was not. Few Europeans stopped to ask questions. For example, was it less civilized for Africans to believe in witches and magic than for Europeans to slaughter hundreds of thousands of people with the aid of modern weapons, the products of their more advanced society?

Europeans criticised without always understanding the African way of life. European missionaries were against *polygamy*, the practice of taking more than one wife. This was common in Africa where it played a part in developing the *extended family*. The extended family consists not merely of parents and children; but of grandparents and their brothers and sisters; a father and his wives and their brothers and sisters; the children and all their cousins. *(The Family)** One idea behind the extended family is that everything should be shared. The result is that few Africans are destitute and lonely. In 'civilized' Europe loneliness, especially of old people, is a major problem. (D1–2)**

Europeans were too hasty with their judgments. It is now certain that Africa and its people played a leading part in the early history of man and his first basic steps towards more settled living. The earliest creatures who can be identified as man's ancestors lived in East Africa. It is man's ability to make and to use tools that distinguishes him from other living creatures. The earliest tool makers so far known lived in Kenya and Tanzania. The rough tools used by these ancestors of modern man, known as hand axes, are more plentiful in Africa than anywhere else. For this reason Africa has been called 'the cradle of man'.

AFRICA'S GEOGRAPHY

To understand African history it is important to know about the geography of the continent. Most of Africa falls into one of three main types of region. Each of these has a particular type of climate and plant life.

First are the deserts, the most important being the Sahara in the north and the Kalahari in the south west. In complete contrast are the tropical forests. The greatest expanses lie along the Guinea coast of West Africa; and in the Congo basin where they extend from the Atlantic coast

*Titles in brackets refer to other booklets in the Program

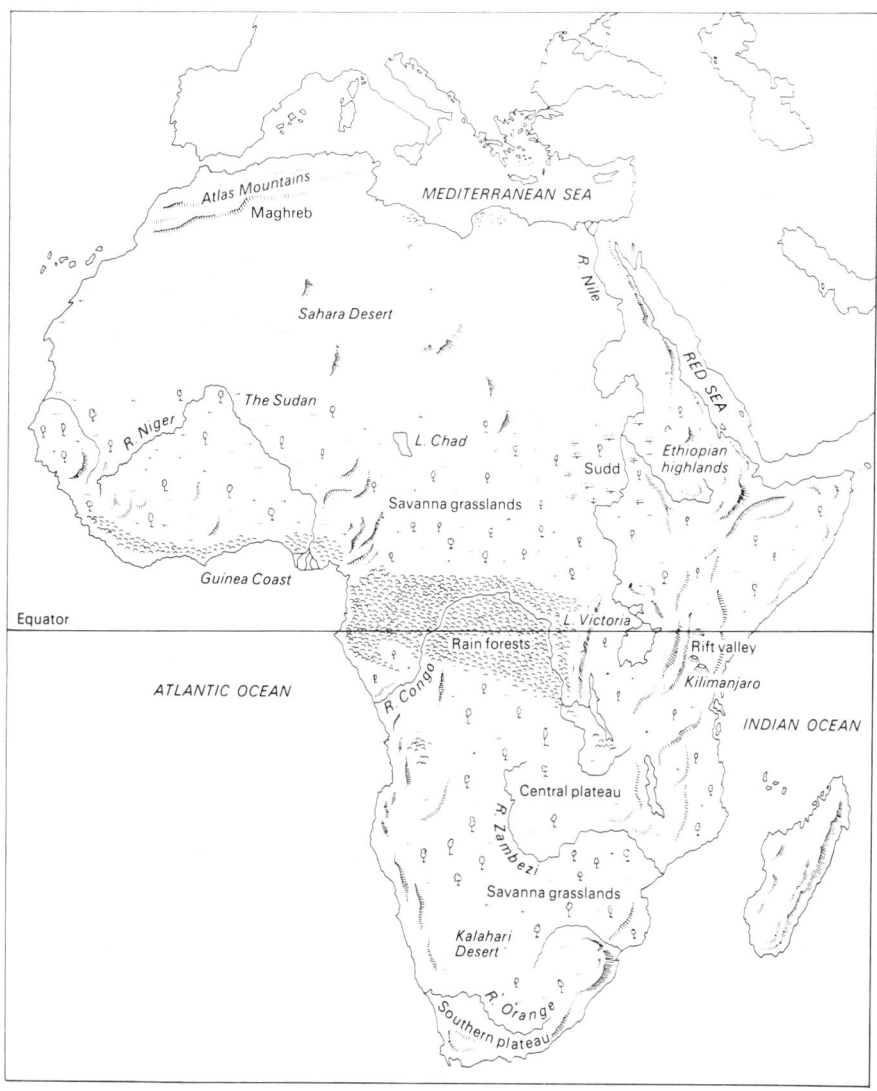

Africa: land and climate

almost to the great lakes of East Africa. In between the dry, plantless deserts and the wet, lush forests are the *savannah* lands. Here plant growth varies from thick woodland to dry scrubland. Here are to be found the best farming lands in Africa. In these lands most of Africa's peoples have always lived; movement is comparatively easy; trade first flourished and almost all of Africa's early states grew up.

Most of Africa south of the equator is a plateau at least 3,000 feet above sea level with very narrow coastal plains. The steep edges of these plateaus explain why none of Africa's main rivers provides an easy way into the

**The reference (D) indicates the numbered documents at the end of this book.

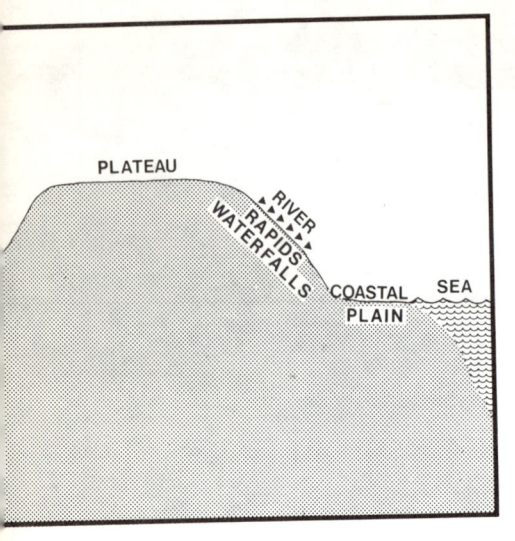

Diagram of the African plateau

interior. The height of much of the continent also explains why much of tropical Africa is not unbearably hot and steamy. East Africa's highest mountains like Kilimanjaro and Mount Kenya are always snow-capped though they are on or very near to the equator. Two gashes in the earth's crust run through much of the eastern half of the continent. These are the Rift Valleys. In these valleys lie a number of great lakes. Near to them are many volcanoes. The soil in and around these is some of the richest in this region. In the north east of the continent, Africa's greatest river, the Nile, lays down through the desert a narrow strip of some of the most fertile soil in the world.

Finally it is well to remember the vast size of Africa. It is 5,000 miles from the Cape of Good Hope to the Mediterranean; and the same distance from the Horn of Africa to the Atlantic. Even the narrower part of the continent is 2,000 miles or more from east to west for most of its length. Distance alone has made communication difficult between one part of Africa and another, until the present century. Barriers like dense forest, desert and unnavigable rivers increased problems of movement.

FARMING AND METALWORKING

In the rest of this booklet we will learn a little about some of the best organised of Africa's early societies and states. It is important to remember that there were others; and, equally important, that there were many African peoples who never developed kingdoms and empires. Examples of ones like these are the Ibo of Nigeria (D13) and the Kikuyu of Kenya.

Man's two most important steps towards organised, settled living were probably learning to farm *(The Neolithic Revolution)* and learning to use metals. Neither of these steps were first taken in Africa; but Africans were not far behind the pioneers. Farming probably began in western Asia, near Jericho, about 8,000 B.C. The first farmers in Africa are found in the lower Nile valley 2–3,00 years later. Here the soil was so fertile that the benefits of farming were felt quickly. Food supplies became more certain. Population grew rapidly. Men could live together in larger groups. Villages and towns appeared. The whole population was not needed to produce food, so some men could become craftsmen and artists and produce things that made life pleasanter. Surplus

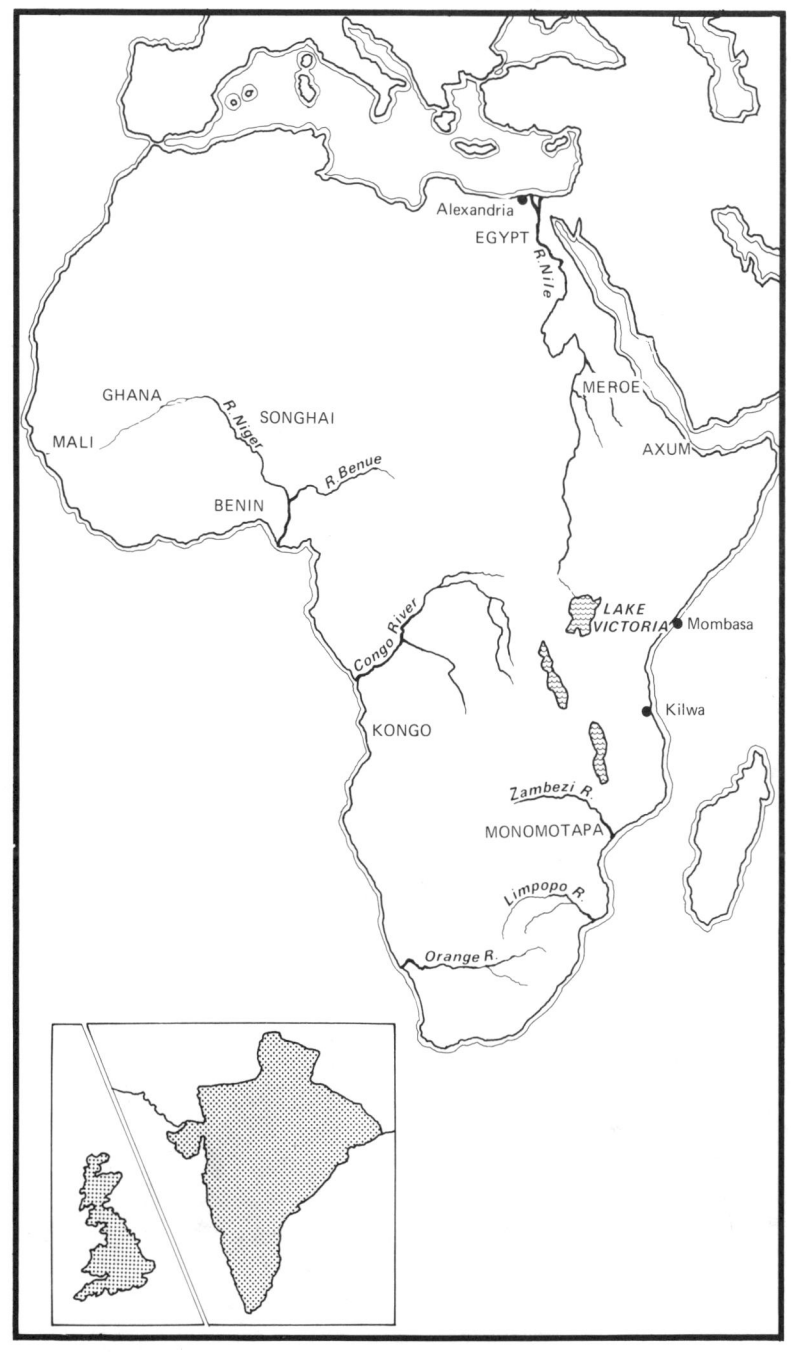

Map of traditional Africa showing the kingdoms and cities. Notice the size of Africa in comparison to England and India

goods led to trade. Trade spread knowledge and ideas to other people. Leaders were needed to provide protection in case of attack, to organize trade, and to make sure that large numbers of people lived peaceably together. Kings and kingdoms emerged. In ancient Egypt one of the world's most brilliant early civilisations developed.

The discovery of metals came later in man's story. Gold and copper were known and used in Egypt by 3,000 B.C. Much the most important metal, however, from the point of view of man's advance was iron. Its discovery was probably made in Asia Minor about 1,500 B.C. It made better tools and weapons than earlier known metals. It helped to make people better farmers and better fighters, and it explains why in 676 B.C. the Assyrians were able to conquer Lower Egypt.

KUSH: THE IRON KINGDOM

Egypt's rulers at that time came from the kingdom of Kush, further up the Nile valley. Its capital was Napata. Knowledge of farming must have reached the people of Kush from Egypt, for the Nile valley was a natural trade route. The Kushites soon abandoned Egypt to the Assyrians.

The ruined remains of a Kush settlement at Meroe, built 2,000 years ago

They probably took back with them to their own kingdom the knowledge of iron working. The Egyptians had neither iron ore nor the timber for smelting it. The Kushites soon had both. About 540 B.C. they moved their capital to Meroe further south. It lay in more fertile lands between the Nile and one of its branches. Today there are great mounds of slag around Meroe, proof that it was once a great iron making centre. (D4)

For several hundred years Kush was Africa's most powerful kingdom. Archaeologists have uncovered many fine buildings and other remains. They show that this was once a rich kingdom trading with many parts of the world. Temples and pyramids show Egyptian influence; swimming baths and temples, Roman influence. There are water storage tanks like others found in Arabia. A picture of a king riding an elephant suggests links with India since African elephants cannot be trained like that.

Kush was great because of its military strength and its trade. Military power must have grown with the rapid growth of iron working from the fourth century B.C. The goods that have formed Africa's main contribution to long distance trade throughout the ages — ivory, gold, ebony, animal skins, ostrich feathers and slaves — came through Kush. From there they passed down the Nile valley to Egypt and the lands around the Mediterranean. The importance of Kush was ended by an attack from another African kingdom, Axum. This lay to the south east of Kush in the mountains of northern Ethiopia. Its kings had come from across the Red Sea in Arabia. Their power also depended on trade, and rivalry and raiding must have grown between these two states. About 350 A.D. King Aezanes of Axum sent an army against Meroe. Axum was victorious. (D5) Axum became the main state in that part of Africa. Soon after her victory Axum became a Christian country. In the mountains of Ethiopia Christian kings have ruled ever since.

THE SOURCES OF AFRICA'S EARLY HISTORY

Most of the people south of the Sahara desert belong to two groups. In the great belt of savannah between the Sahara and the tropical forests live the West Africans. Over most of the rest of central, eastern and southern Africa the Bantu-speaking peoples are dominant. We can learn a great deal about Africa's early history from the story of how the Bantu-speaking peoples came to occupy most of Africa south of the equator. This story has been pieced together from evidence provided by many different kinds of experts. Linguists studying Africa's 300 Bantu languages believes that all these have developed in not much more than 2,000 years from a single language. The difference between them is a measure of the length of time different groups have been separated from one another. *(Language)* Botanists know that most of the main crops grown today came into Africa from other continents. Bananas and Asian

7

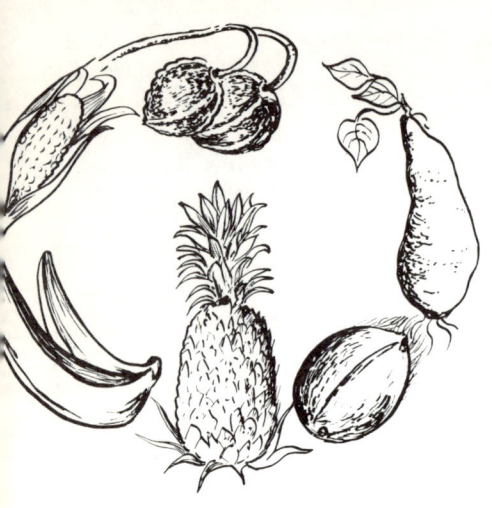

Food crops brought to Africa from other lands: pineapples, bananas, maize, cassavas, yams and coconuts.

yams were brought across the Indian Ocean by Indonesians sometime before 400 A.D. Without these crops large numbers of people could not have survived for long in the wetter parts of Africa. Archaeologists have traced the movements of groups through the evidence of early iron working and certain kinds of pottery. In more recent times, as the last journeys of these groups took them into the less fertile parts of the continent, *oral traditions* add to the story. People who have no written language preserve the story of their past through the spoken word. Africans were in this position until quite recently. Important peoples had *praise singers* or *minstrels* whose job was to preserve the traditional stories in this way.

Thus much of the early history of Africa is written from unusual sources. Few Africans left written records before recent times. But many outsiders who visited or lived in Africa did so. The Greek historian Herodotus was one of the earliest of these. (D4) Another Greek, a sailor from Alexandria, in about 120 A.D. wrote a guide to the Red Sea and to the northern part of the East African coast.

Much of the written evidence about Africa south of the Sahara comes from Arab writers and Muslim Africans writing in Arabic. These writings begin in the tenth century. From the fifteenth century, beginning with the Portuguese, the records of European visitors begin. A few Africans writing in Arabic and later in Swahili add to the growing list from the sixteenth century. Examples of all these written records are included in the documents in the second part of the book.

ANCIENT GHANA, MALI AND SONGHAI: THREE EMPIRES IN WEST AFRICA

When Kush was defeated by Axum in about 350 A.D. it is probable that some Kushites who escaped the slaughter fled westwards across the savannah lands in the direction of Lake Chad. They took with them ideas of kingship and it is possible that they played a part in the growth of the first kingdoms in this part of Africa. These began to develop about 400 A.D.

Traders had used this same route for centuries. Others used the more difficult one across the Sahara from North Africa. Knowledge of farming may have reached the Western Sudan by these routes. But even if it did the

West Africans must have developed their own crops like rice, millet and sorghum. The people of the forest further south developed different crops suited to their climate.

Long before kingdoms appeared the people of this region were not only farming but making sculpture. They made heads and small figures in baked clay. The figures were linked with a form of ancestor worship. The first of them was discovered accidently near the village of Nok in modern Nigeria and the figures have been named after Nok.

When the first Arab historians began to write about the area one of the kings had become more powerful than the rest. This was the King or Emperor of ancient Ghana. (D6) There were two main reasons for his power. His empire lay at the southern end of the important trader routes across the desert and he grew wealthy by controlling this trade. (D7) He also had a large army equipped with iron weapons.

Baked clay head from Nok, about 200 B.C.

The Saharan trade routes had existed for centuries. Trade increased when camels were brought into North Africa from Arabia sometime before 400 A.D. The trade was based largely on two items — salt and gold. There was

A camel being used to carry goods across the Sahara

little salt in the Western Sudan. (The name given to the West African interior). In the Sahara, especially the northern part, salt is plentiful. Gold was found in various parts of West Africa. It was in great demand in Europe and the lands of the Muslim peoples after the seventh century. Arab merchants came to play an important part in the trade and Arab writers have much to say about it. Gold was obtained from the Africans by a process called 'dumb barter'. (D8) The King of Ghana charged duty on all goods entering and leaving his country, and was thus able to keep a splendidly rich court. Though there were Arabs trading with and living in his country he and his subjects kept their African religion. This was shown by the burial ceremony of their kings. (D9) It was similar in some ways to the burial of Egyptian kings.

In 1240, after several hundred years, the rulers of ancient Ghana lost their supremacy to the kings of the little state of Mali. Military power, and with it control of the vital trade routes, passed into the hands of Sundiata, king of Mali. (D10) Just over two hundred years later, in 1460, a second takeover, for the same reasons, was made by Sunni Ali. He was king of Songhai, a people who lived several hundred miles down the river Niger from Mali. He had a great fleet of war canoes as well as a powerful army. He became the new overlord of the region and the founder of the Songhai Empire. These later empires were larger, wealthier and more powerful than Ghana. Ibn Battuta, the greatest of all the Arab travellers and writers described the lavish ceremonies that took place at the court of Mali. (D11) Trade and military power still made these states important; but the religion of Islam now had great influence. Most of the rulers and their leading subjects were Muslims. Great mosques built on the baked clay of the region began to appear in places like Timbuktu and Djenne. The rulers went on pilgrimages to Mecca. *(Muhammad and the Arab Empire)* Mansa Musa the greatest of the rulers of Mali (1302–1337 A.D.) made the pilgrimage in 1324. He was accompanied by five hundred servants and about a hundred camels loaded with gold and other valuables as gifts. (D12) After his pilgrimage he became well known outside his own country and he appears on a famous map drawn by a Spanish geographer. Ibn Battuta visited his capital in 1352 and was delighted to find that so many people were good Muslims. (D13) By the sixteenth century Djenne and Timbuktu were well known places of learning and Timbuktu had a university attended by students from different parts of the Muslim world. (D14–15)

The great days of the western Sudan ended suddenly in 1509. A Moroccan army, equipped with firearms which the army of Songhai did not possess, conquered Songhai, whose power collapsed, but the Moroccans were unable to control the country at such a distance from home.

Mecca is still the religious centre of the Muslim world

Mansa Musa, the Emperor of Mali, shown on a Spanish map drawn in 1375. He is holding a large nugget of gold

THE KINGDOM OF BENIN: A FOREST STATE

For several hundred years the traders from the empires of the savannah had links with the peoples of the forest to the south. This trade led to the rise of states in the forest and at the coast. We have no written records about these states until the arrival of the Portuguese on the Guinea coast about 1470. What we know about them has been learned largely from oral tradition.

Benin was the most famous of the early forest states. Its traditional history goes back as far

Head of the Oni (King) of Ife. Made in the thirteenth century by the 'lost wax process'

Cast bronze head of the Queen Mother (iyoba). Made in Benin in the early sixteenth century

as the twelfth century. At this time the people of Benin asked the king or *Oni* of Ife to send one of his sons to rule in Benin. This was

Bronze plaques made in Benin in the late sixteenth century and used to decorate the Royal Palace

done and since that time the ruler of Benin has been known as the *Oba*. Both Ife and Benin were famous for their works of art. These were usually sculpted in brass by the *lost wax process*. It worked like this. A wax model of the subject was made on a clay base. The whole was then covered with wet clay, with a few pieces of wax left sticking through the clay, dried and set hard. Heat was applied to melt the wax which was poured away. The clay formed a mould into which molten metal was poured. When the metal had set the clay was carefully broken away.

Early relations between Europeans and the people of Benin were friendly. The Portuguese sent missionaries at the request of the Oba. The merchants of Benin were clever traders. (D16) All Europeans were impressed by the city of Benin and particularly by the large and splendid royal palace. (D17) Round the walls of the palace were many bronze plaques telling the story of Benin's past. Ivory was another material in which the craftsmen of Benin produced beautiful works of art. The decline of Benin began with the rapid increase of the slave trade in the seventeenth century. *(The Slave Trade)*

THE KINGDOM OF KONGO

In 1482 the first Portuguese ship sailed into the estuary of the river Congo. Three years later the second expedition sailed further up the estuary and found another of Africa's well organised kingdoms. This was the kingdom of Kongo. It lay south of the river and was ruled by a king with the title of Manikongo. At first, as at Benin, relations between the Portuguese and the African ruler were good. Missionaries arrived and the Manikongo was converted. The Portuguese sent carpenters, masons and other skilled craftsmen. In 1507 a new Manikongo came to the throne. He was baptised and took the Christian name Affonso. Hopes ran high that the King of Portugal would continue to send skilled men to Kongo. However, the Portuguese had by this time

Ivory mask carved by the craftsmen of Benin in the early sixteenth century

Captured slaves being taken to the coast

set up large farms and plantations on two islands north of the Congo estuary. Slaves were taken from Kongo to work on the plantations. Soon even greater demands for slaves came from Portugal's colony of Brazil across the Atlantic. *(The Slave Trade)* By 1526 Affonso saw clearly how slave trading was draining his kingdom of its best men and women. Worst still, Portuguese traders were undermining his authority with his nobles by trading with them against his orders. He sent desperate letters begging the King of Portugal to stop the slave trade which was ruining his kingdom. (D18) By the time of Affonso's death in 1545 Kongo was in a state of disorder. The Portuguese were already losing interest in it and looking further south in Angola for their slaves.

TRADING CITIES OF THE EAST AFRICAN COAST

In 1489 Vasco da Gama, the Portuguese explorer, rounded the Cape of Good Hope and sailed up the east African coast. He found many ports all engaged in the rich trading network of the Indian Ocean. They had trading links with all the lands round the Indian Ocean and beyond to the Spice Islands, Thailand and China. Most of this trade was controlled by Muslim merchants. The Portuguese were surprised at the wealth of the ports and their inhabitants. At Malinda, one of the city ports, Vasco da Gama was given a friendly reception and a pilot to take him to the west coast of India. After his return home the Portuguese decided that the East African towns would have to be conquered if they wished to

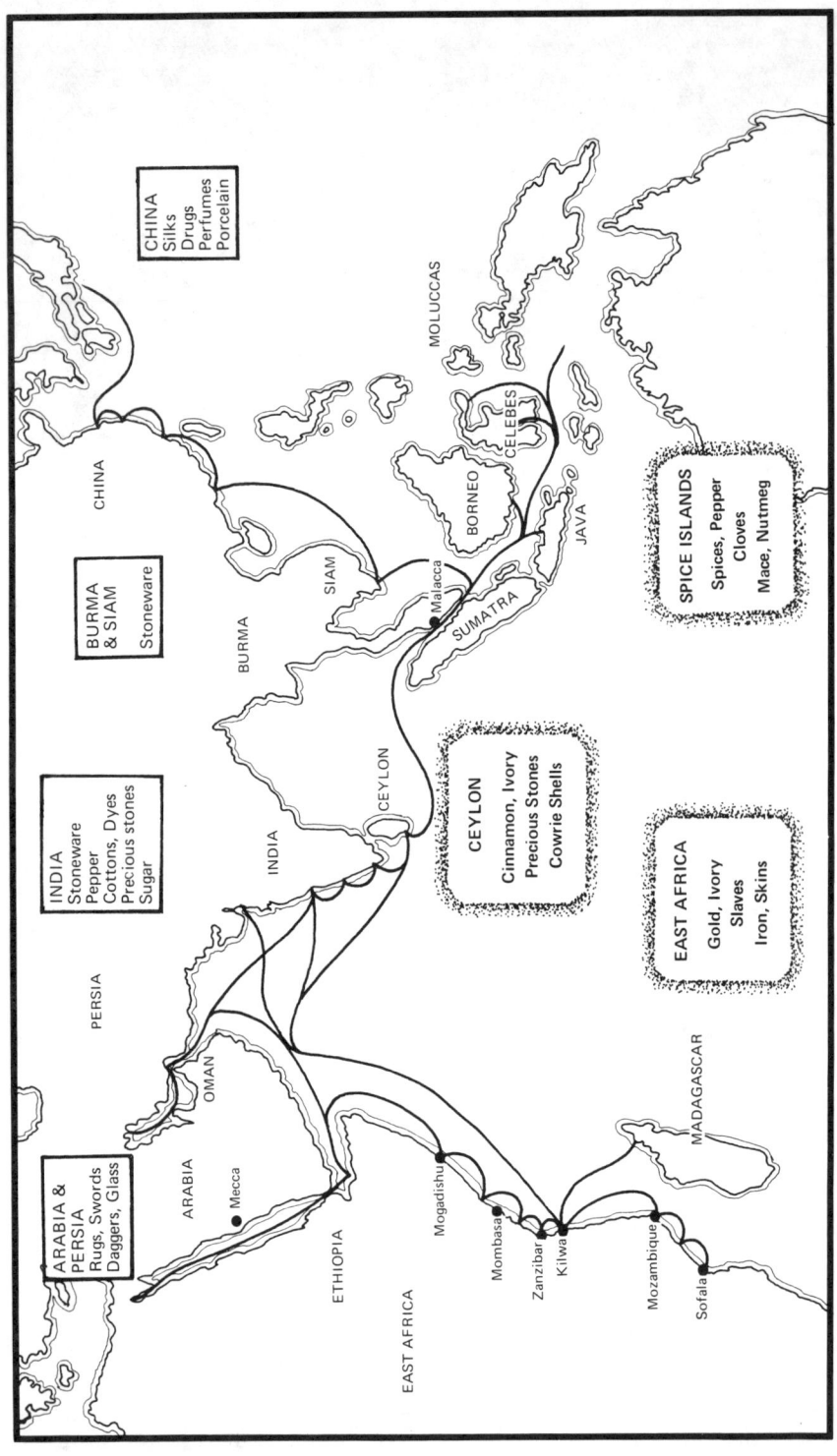

Indian Ocean trade routes

Fort Jesus, Mombasa, built by the Portuguese in 1593

This Portuguese map of Mombasa Island shows Fort Jesus guarding the entrance to the harbour

control the rich Indian Ocean trade for themselves and have ports of call on the way to India and the Spice Islands. *(Spices and Civilizations)*.

By 1509, thanks largely to their better ships, better guns and better trained soldiers, the Portuguese had crushed the resistance of the people of the coast. Prosperous places like Kilwa and Mombasa were looted and burned.

The prosperity which the Portuguese found on their first few visits was the result of many centuries of slow growth. Before the birth of Christ, Egyptians, Arabs and Greeks had visited the coast for trade. But the coast's real importance began with the visits of Arabs and other Muslim peoples after 700 A.D. Some of these settled on the coast, and married locally. As a result a new people and new language gradually grew up. The Arabs used the word Swahili, meaning coast, to describe the people, the language and the culture. But this civilisation was never united. The different towns had their own rulers, mainly Arab and Swahili. From 1100 A.D. Arab influence grew rapidly all round the Indian Ocean. Mosques were built all along the coast. Some of these like the great Mosque at Kilwa were fine buildings in stone. Ibn Battuta who visited the coast in 1331 was pleased to find Islam so strong. He was impressed by the well built towns and their well-dressed and well-fed inhabitants.

By this time Kilwa was the richest and most powerful place on the coast. It had a central position. Long-distance ships from Persia and India relied on the monsoon winds. They were brought to East Africa by the north east monsoon. Few dared to sail further than Kilwa for fear of missing the south west monsoon which took them home again. The coastal Arab *dhows* (sailing boats) with gold from Sofala had to call here. The Sultans of Kilwa collected customs duties from all merchants who used the port. (D19) The accounts of Arabs and early Portuguese visitors (D20–21) and the discovery of coins, pottery etc. tell of the wealth of these towns and of their trade over a wide area.

The Great Mosque at Kilwa. Built in the thirteenth century and enlarged in the early fifteenth century

An Arab dhow, used for centuries as a trading vessel between East Africa and other parts of the Indian Ocean

THE KINGDOM OF THE MONOMOTAPA

It was the gold trade at Sofala and Kilwa that the Portuguese were most anxious to control. They learned from Arabs at the coast that the gold came from the lands of a ruler called the Monomotapa. A ruler with this title had brought most of what is now Rhodesia under his control by the early fifteenth century. He had his capital at Great Zimbabwe. There were many *zimbabwes* or royal dwellings. This one consists of two sites separated from each other by about a quarter of a mile. One is now called the Temple site and the other the Acropolis. The Temple is oval shaped, about 300 feet by 200 feet, and enclosed by a massive stone wall thirty feet high. Inside are the remains of several buildings including a conical shaped tower. It contained the royal palace where the king, his wives and his officials lived. The Acropolis is a rocky site. The natural rocks have been skilfully linked by stone walls to form a defensive stronghold. The buildings were begun in the twelfth century but others, including the great wall and the tower belong to the seventeenth century.

The Monomotapa was a divine

The Temple site at the Great Zimbabwe, built to enclose the Royal Palace

The Acropolis site at the Great Zimbabwe, built for defence

king. He was not seen by his ordinary subjects but gave interviews from behind a screen. If he fell ill he was expected to commit suicide to make way for a younger, fitter ruler. (D22) A constantly burning fire was a symbol of his authority over lesser kings. It was put out only on the death of the Monomotapa. Each year it was used to re-light the fires of his subject kings (D23)

Just before the arrival of the Portuguese there was an argument about the succession to the throne. New rulers, the Changamires, seized Great Zimbabwe and controlled the main gold mining area. The Portuguese never succeeded in entering their kingdom. The Monomotapa was left with the northern part of the kingdom and had his capital in the Zambesi valley. In 1629 the Portuguese chose as Monomotapa, a man called Mavura who did what they told him and signed a treaty giving them many privileges. (D24) The people of the coast, Arabs, Swahili and Africans hated the Portuguese. Wars and rebellions were frequent. As a result the trade dwindled and almost died. By 1698 the Portuguese had been forced to withdraw from the part of the coast north of modern Mozambique. They had introduced some new tropical crops like maize, cassava and the sweet potato. Otherwise their presence had been largely destructive.

THE IMPORTANCE OF AFRICA'S EARLY HISTORY

Only a small part of Africa's early history has been sketched here. We have looked at some of the old kingdoms and trading cities. It is important to remember that there were many African peoples who did not develop kingdoms. More of their history is being discovered every day. The early history of Africa gives us a very good chance to study some of the things that have influenced man's development. These include geography and climate; learning about farming and metal working; the growth of population and organised states. We can see too how states decline more quickly than they grow. Amongst the reasons for such decline has been the lack of understanding of Africa by conquerors from outside. One of the first British colonial governors in East Africa said, 'We have in East Africa the rare experience of . . . an almost untouched country where we can do as we will'.

The leaders of Africa's independent states today know that it is important to remember their past, and to learn from it.

DOCUMENT 1

AN AFRICAN FAMILY   BABA — *A woman of the Muslim Hausa of Northern Nigeria who was born in 1890, dictated the story of her life*

They all farmed, our family have no other craft to this day except farming; one or two of them weave, but most of them dislike weaving. After my grandfather died, each son farmed on his own, but on market-day all the brothers went to market together to trade. When they came home we children were happy — 'Father has come home! Welcome home, Father!' Our father gave us fine things, rings and bangles and cloth. His younger sister made stew for us. His elder brother was Malam Buhari. Their compounds were close, close together. Malam Baya was there with his wives, Maria and Iya — he was a younger brother of our grandfather Dara. There were about thirty compounds belonging to our family. 'Tantabara's father has come home' — 'Fari Biyar's father has come home' — 'Danda's father has come home' — that was our own father. That is what we called our fathers. We grew up with all their children.

DOCUMENT 2

A FAMILY COMPOUND IN IBOLAND (SOUTHEAST NIGERIA)
OLAUDAH EQUIANO — An eighteenth-century African

... Each master of a family has a large square piece of ground, surrounded with a moat or fence, or enclosed with a wall made of red earth tempered, which, when dry, is as hard as brick. Within this are his houses to accommodate his family and slaves; which, if numerous, frequently present the appearance of a village. In the middle stands the principal building, appropriated to the sole use of the master, and consisting of two apartments; in one of which he sits in the day with his family, the other is left apart for the reception of his friends. He has besides these a distinct apartment, in which he sleeps, with his male children. On each side are the apartments of his wives, who have also their separate day and night houses. The habitations of the slaves and their families are distributed throughout the rest of the enclosure. These houses never exceed one storey in height; they are always built of wood, of stakes driven into the ground, crossed with wattles, and neatly plastered within and without. The roof is thatched with reeds. Our day houses are left open at the sides; but those in which we sleep are always covered and plastered in the inside with a composition mixed with cow dung, to keep off the different insects which annoy us during the night.

DOCUMENT 3

SOCIAL ORGANIZATION AND GOVERNMENT AMONGST THE IBO
OLAUDAH EQUIANO

... The distance of this province from the capital of Benin and the sea must be very considerable; for I had never heard of white men or Europeans, nor of the sea; and our subjection to the king of Benin was no more than nominal; for every transaction of the government, as far as my slender observation extended, was conducted by the chiefs or elders of the place. The manners and government of a people who have little commerce with other countries are generally very simple; and the history of what passes in one family or village, may serve as a specimen of the whole nation. My father was one of those elders or chiefs and was styled Embrenché; a term as I remember, importing the highest distinction, and signifying in our language a mark of grandeur. This mark is conferred on the person entitled to it, by cutting the skin across at the top of the forehead, and drawing it down to the eyebrows; and while it is in this situation, applying a warm hand, and rubbing it until it shrinks up into a thick weal across the lower part of the forehead. Most of the judges and senators were thus marked ... Those Embrenché, or chief men, decided disputes, and punished crimes; for which purpose they always assembled together.

DOCUMENT 4

MEROE   *HERODOTUS – The Greek historian describes the city in 430 B.C.*

At this point one must land and travel along the bank of the river for forty days, because sharp rocks, some showing above the water and many just awash, make the river impracticable for boats. After forty days' journey on land one takes another boat and in twelve days reaches a big city named Meroe, said to be the capital city of the Ethiopians. The inhabitants worship Zeus and Dionysus alone of the Gods, holding them in great honour. There is an oracle of Zeus there, and they make war according to its pronouncements, taking from it both the occasion and the object of their various expeditions.

DOCUMENT 5

KING AEZANES DEFEATS THE KUSHITES   *From an inscription at Axum probably made by the King in about 350 A.D.*

Twice or thrice they had broken their solemn oaths, and had killed their neighbours without mercy, and they had stripped our deputies and messengers whom I sent to enquire into their raids, and had stolen their weapons and belongings. And as I had warned them, and they would not listen but refused to cease from their evil deeds and betook themselves to flight, I made war on them ... They fled without making a stand, and I pursued them for twenty-three days, killing some and capturing others ... I burnt their towns ... and my armies carried off their food and copper and iron ... and destroyed the statues in their temples, their granaries, and cotton trees and cast them into the River Seda (Nile).

DOCUMENT 6

GHANA IN 1067 *AL BEKRI – An Arab traveller*

Ghana is the title of the kings of this people ... The king who governs them at present ... is called Tenkaminen; he came to the throne in AH 455 (1067 A.D.) ... Tenkaminen is the master of a large empire and a formidable power ... The king of Ghana can put two hundred thousand warriors in the field, more than forty thousand being armed with bow and arrow ...

When he gives audience to his people, to listen to their complaints and set them to rights, he sits in a pavilion around which stand ten pages holding shields and gold-mounted swords: and on his right hand are the sons of the princes of his empire, splendidly clad and with gold plaited into their hair. The Governor of the city is seated on the ground in front of the king, and all around him are the vizirs in the same position. The gate of the chamber is guarded by dogs of an excellent breed, who never leave the king's seat: they wear collars of gold and silver, ornamented with the same metals. The beginning of a royal audience is announced by the beating of a kind of drum which they call *deba,* made of a long piece of hollowed wood. The people gather when they hear this sound.

DOCUMENT 7

HOW THE KING OF GHANA RAISES MONEY THROUGH TRADE
AL BEKRI

The King (of Ghana) exacts the right of one *dinar* of gold on each donkey load of salt that enters his country, and two *dinars* of gold on each load of salt that goes out. A load of copper carries a duty of five *mitqals* and a load of merchandise ten *mitqals.* The best gold in the country came from Ghiaru, a town situated eighteen days journey from the capital in a country that is densely populated by negroes and covered with villages. All pieces of native gold found in the mines of the empire belong to the sovereign, although he lets the public have the gold dust everybody knows about; without this precaution gold would become so abundant as practically to lose its value.

DOCUMENT 8

DUMB BARTER   *AL MAS'UDI — Another Arab writer who travelled in the tenth century describes the bartering for gold*

The kingdom of Ghana is one of great importance and it adjoins the land of the gold mines. Great peoples of the Sudan live there . . . They have traced a boundary which no one who sets out to them ever crosses. When the merchants reach this boundary, they place their wares and cloth on the ground and then depart, and so the people of the Sudan come bearing gold which they leave beside the merchandise and then depart. The owners of the merchandise then return, and if they are satisfied with what they have found, they take it. If not, they go away again, and the people of the Sudan return and add to the price until the bargain is concluded. The visiting merchants beat drums to let the gold diggers know of their arrival; and these are beaten again when they are finally satisfied with the gold which has been offered.

DOCUMENT 9

THE BURIAL OF A KING OF GHANA   *AL BEKRI*

When the king dies they build over the place where his tomb will be an enormous dome of wood. They bring him in a bed and place him inside the dome. At his side they place his ornaments, his weapons and the vessels from which he used to eat and drink. They also place there the man who used to serve his meals. They close the doors of the dome and cover it with mats and materials and then they assemble the people, who heap earth upon it until it becomes like a large mound. Then they dig a ditch round the mound until it can be reached at only one place. They sacrifice victims for their dead and make offerings of intoxicating drinks.

DOCUMENT 10

THE MILITARY VICTORY OF SUNDIATA, KING OF MALI, OVER SOUMAORO, KING OF SOSSO AND GHANA   *MAMADOU KOUYATA — A present day bard tells this story which has been handed down for hundreds of years*

I am a *griot* (bard). It is I, Djeli Mamadou Kouyate. Since time immemorial the Kouyates have been in the service of the princes of Mali; we are vessels of speech, we are the repositories which harbour secrets many centuries old. . .

I am going to tell you of Sundiata. He was a great man among kings; he was beloved of God.

Sundiata wanted to have done with Soumaoro before the rainy season, so he struck camp and marched on Soumaoro . . . With his powerful voice Sundiata cried, 'An gnewa' (forward!) The order was repeated from tribe to tribe and the army started off. His eyes red with anger, Sundiata pulled his cavalry over to the left in the direction of the hills . . . The king of Sosso, who did not want Sundiata to get near him, retreated far behind his men, but Sundiata followed him with his eyes. He stopped and bent his body. The arrow flew and grazed Soumaoro on the shoulder. The effect was immediate and Soumaoro felt his powers leave him. His eyes met Sundiata's. Now trembling like a man in the grip of a fever, the vanquished Soumaoro looked up towards the sun. A great black bird flew over above the fray and he understood. It was a bird of misfortune. The king of Sosso let out a great cry and, turning his horse's head, he took to flight. The Sossos saw the king and fled in their turn. It was a rout. Death hovered over the great plain and blood poured out of a thousand wounds. From everywhere around the kings sent their submission to Sundiata. Sosso vanished from the earth and it was Sundiata . . . who gave these places over to solitude. After the destruction of Soumaoro's capital the world knew no other master but Sundiata.

DOCUMENT 11

A RELIGIOUS FESTIVAL AT THE COURT OF THE SULTAN OF MALI   IBN BATTUTA — *A fourteenth-century Arab traveller*

I was at Mali during the two festivals of the sacrifice and the fast-breaking. On these days the sultan takes his seat on the *pempi* (platform) after the mid-afternoon prayer . . . The armour-bearers bring in magnificent arms — quivers of gold and silver, swords ornamented with gold and with golden scabbards, gold and silver lances, and crystal maces. At his head stand four *amirs* driving off the flies, having in their hands silver ornaments resembling saddle stirrups. The commanders and preacher sit in their usual places. The interpreter, Dugha, comes with his four wives and his slave girls, who are about a hundred in number. They are wearing beautiful robes, and on their heads they have gold and silver filets, with gold and silver balls attached. A chair is placed for Dugha to sit on. He plays on an instrument made of reeds, with some small calabashes at its lower end, and chants a poem in praise of the sultan, recalling his battles and deeds of valour. The women and girls sing along with him and play with bows. Accompanying them are about thirty youths, wearing red woollen tunics and white skull caps; each of them has a drum slung from his shoulder and beats it. Afterward come his boy pupils who play and turn wheels in the air, like the natives of Sind. They show a marvellous nimbleness and agility in these exercises, and play most cleverly with swords . . .

On feast-days, after Dugha has finished his display, the poets come in. Each of them is inside a figure resembling a thrush, made of feathers, and provided with a wooden head with a red beak, to look like a thrush's head. They stand in front of the sultan in this ridiculous make-up and recite their poems.

DOCUMENT 12

THE VALUE OF MONEY FALLS IN CAIRO   *AL OMARI – An Arab writer describes the result of the distribution of gold by Sultan Mansa Musa of Mali in 1324*

'This man', el Mehmendar told me, 'spread upon Cairo the flood of his generosity: there was no person, officer of the (Cairo) court or holder of any office of the (Cairo) sultanate who did not receive a sum in gold from him. The people of Cairo earned incalculable sums from him, whether by buying and selling or by gifts. So much gold was current in Cairo that it ruined the value of money.'

DOCUMENT 13

THE PEOPLE OF MALI   *IBN BATTUTA*

Among the admirable qualities of these people the following are to be noted:
　The small number of acts of injustice that one finds there; for the Negroes are of all peoples those who most abhor injustice. The sultan pardons no one who is guilty of it.
　The complete and general safety one enjoys throughout the land. The traveller has no more reason than the man who stays at home to fear brigands, thieves or ravishers . . .
　They make their prayers punctually; they assiduously attend their meetings of the faithful and punish their children if these should fail in this. On Fridays, anyone who is late at the mosque will find nowhere to pray, the crowd is so great.
　They zealously learn the Koran by heart. Those children who are neglectful in this are put in chains until they have memorized the Koran.

DOCUMENT 14

TIMBUKTU IN 1526   *LEO AFRICANUS – An Arab from Spain who travelled in the sixteenth century*

Corn, cattle, milk, and butter this region yieldeth in great abundance: but salt is very scarce here; for it is brought hither by land from Taghaza which is 500 miles distant. When I myself was here, I saw one camel's load of salt sold for 80 ducats . . .
　Here are great store of doctors, judges, priests, and other learned men, that are bountifully maintained at the king's cost and charges, and hither are brought divers manuscripts or written books out of Barbary, which are sold for more money than any other merchandise. The coin of Timbuktu is of gold without any stamp or superscription: but in matters of small value they use certain shells brought hither out of the kingdom

of Persia . . . The inhabitants are people of gentle and cheerful disposition, and spend a great part of the night singing and dancing through all the streets of the city.

DOCUMENT 15

LEARNING IN TIMBUKTU IN THE SIXTEENTH CENTURY
MAHMUD KATI – An Arab historian

In those days Timbuktu did not have its equal – from the province of Mali to the extreme limits of the region of the Maghrib – for the solidity of its institutions . . . its courtesy towards students and men of learning and the financial assistance which it provided for the latter: the scholars of this period were the most respected among the believers for their generosity, force of character and their discretion.

DOCUMENT 16

THE BENIN MERCHANTS   *SIXTEENTH-CENTURY ENGLISH TRADER*

They are very wary people in their bargaining, and will not lose one spark of gold of any value. They use weights and measures, and are very circumspect in occupying the same. They that shall have to do with them, must use them gently; for they will not traffic or bring in any wares, if they be evilly used. At the first voyage, that our men had into these parts, it so chanced that, at their departure from the first place where they did traffic, one of them either stole a musk-cat, or took her away by force, not mistrusting that that should have hindered their bargaining in another place whither they intended to go. But for all the haste they could make with full sails, the fame of their mis-usage so prevented (went before) them that the people of that place also, offended thereby, would bring in no wares; insomuch that they were enforced either to restore the cat, or pay for her at their price, before they could traffic there.

DOCUMENT 17

BENIN CITY AND THE ROYAL PALACE IN THE SEVENTEENTH CENTURY   *OLFERT DAPPER – A Dutch writer*

The town seems to be very great; when you enter into it, you go into a great broad street, not paved, which seems to be seven or eight times broader than the Warmoes street in Amsterdam . . .

    The King's Court is very great, within it having many great foursquare plains, which round about them have galleries, wherein there is always watch kept. I was so far within the Court that I passed over four such great plains, and wherever I looked, still I saw gates upon gates to go into other places . . . I went so far as any Netherlander was, which was to the stable where his best horses stood, always passing a great long way. It seems that the King has many soldiers; he has also many gentlemen, who when they come to the court ride on horses . . . There are also many men slaves seen in the town, that carry water, yams, and palm-wine, which they say is for the King; and many carry grass, which is for their horses; and all this is carried to the Court.

DOCUMENT 18

THE SLAVE TRADE IN KONGO *KING AFFONSO OF KONGO – In a letter of 1526 to King John of Portugal begging him to stop his merchants trading in slaves*

And we cannot reckon how great the damage is, since the mentioned merchants are taking every day our natives, sons of the land and the sons of our noblemen and vassals and our relatives . . . ; they grab them and get them to be sold; and so great, Sir, is the corruption and licentiousness that our country is being completely depopulated . . . And to avoid it we need from your Kingdom no more than some priests and a few people to teach in schools, and no other goods except wine and flour for the Holy Sacrament. That is why we beg of Your Highness to help and assist us in this matter, commanding your agents that they should not send here either merchants or wares, because it is *our will that in these Kingdoms there shall not be any trade of slaves nor outlet for them.* Concerning what is mentioned above, again we beg of Your Highness to agree with it, since otherwise we cannot remedy such an obvious damage.

DOCUMENT 19

CUSTOMS DUTIES AT KILWA *DIOGO DE ALCANCOVA – From a letter written to the King of Portugal in 1506*

And duties which the king of Kilwa has are: that any merchant who wishes to enter the city pays for each five hundred pieces of cloth he brings, no matter what the quality, one *mitqal* of gold as entrance duty; and after paying this *mitqal* for the five hundred pieces of cloth, the king takes two-thirds of all the merchandise, and the merchant one-third; and the third which remains to the merchant must not be taken from the city, and the whole merchandise remaining in that third is again valued, and pays for each thousand *mitqals* thirty *mitqals* for the king of Kilwa. And from that place the merchant departs for Sofala; and on arriving there, he must pay for every seven pieces of cloth one piece for the said king of Kilwa. And when anyone returns from Sofala, he is obliged to stop at Kilwa; and he must pay to the king for each thousand mitqals of gold he carries with him fifty mitqals of gold.

DOCUMENT 20

KILWA IN 1500   *DUARTE BARBOSA — A sixteenth-century trade official*

Going along the coast from this town of Mozambique, there is an island hard by the mainland which is called Kilwa, in which is a Moorish town with many fair houses of stones and mortar, with many windows after our fashion, very well arranged in streets, with many flat roofs. The doors are of wood, well carved, with excellent joinery. Around it are streams and orchards and fruit gardens ... It has a Moorish king over it. From this place they trade with Sofala, whence they bring back gold ...

And in this town was great plenty of gold, as no ships passed towards Sofala without first coming to this island. Of the Moors there are some fair and some black, they are finely clad in rich garments of gold and silk and cotton, and the women as well; also with much gold and silver in chains and bracelets, which they wear on their legs and arms, and many jewelled earrings in their ears.

DOCUMENT 21

MOMBASA IN 1500   *DUARTE BARBOSA*

Further on, an advance along the coast towards India, there is an isle hard by the mainland, on which is a town called Mombasa. It is a very fair place, with lofty stone and mortar houses, well aligned in streets after the fashion of Kilwa. The wood is well fitted with excellent joiner's work. It has its own king, himself a Moor. The men are in colour either tawny, black or white and also their women go very bravely attired with many fine garments of silk and gold in abundance. This is a place of great traffic, and has a good harbour, in which are always moored craft of many kinds and also great ships, both those which come from Sofala and those which go thither, and others which come from the great kingdom of Cambay (India) and Malindi; others which sail to the isles of Zanzibar ...

This Mombasa is a land very full of food. There are found many very fine sheep with round tails, cows and other cattle in great plenty, and many fowls, all of which are exceeding fat. There is much millet and rice, sweet and bitter oranges, lemons, pomegranates, Indian figs, vegetables of divers kinds, and much sweet water. The men thereof are oft-times at war but seldom at peace with those of the mainland, and they carry on trade with them, bringing thence great store of honey, wax and ivory.

DOCUMENT 22

THE SUICIDE OF THE MONOMOTAPA   *JOAO DOS SANTOS – A Portuguese priest who travelled in Central Africa in the late sixteenth century*

Anciently the Kings were wont to drink poison in any grievous disasters, as in a contagious disease, or natural impotency, lameness, the loss of their fore-teeth, or other deformities; saying, that Kings ought to have no defect; which if it happened, it was honour to die, and go to better himself in that better life, in which he should be wholly perfect.

DOCUMENT 23

THE VASSAL KINGS LIGHT THEIR FIRES FROM THAT OF THE MONOMOTAPA   *DUARTE BARBOSA*

The king of Monomotapa every year sends men of rank from his kingdom to all the seignories and places which he holds, to give them new fire, that he may know whether they are obedient to him, in this wise. Each of these men when he arrives at each town has every fire put out, so that not one fire is left in the place. And when all are out, they all come and receive fire from his hand in token of the greatest friendship and obedience. So much so, that the place or town which is not willing to do so is forthwith accused of rebellion. Thereupon the king at once sends his aforesaid captain, who either destroys the seigniory or reduces it to subjection. This captain, with all his warriors, wheresoever he wishes to stay, is fed at the cost of the town. Their provisions are millet, rice, and flesh.

DOCUMENT 24

THE TREATY BETWEEN THE MONOMOTAPA AND THE KING OF PORTUGAL IN 1629

First that this kingdom is delivered to him (i.e. to Mavura) in the name of the king of Portugal, our lord, of whom he shall acknowledge himself to be a vassal . . .

That he, the said king, shall allow all the religious of whatever order who may be in his *zimbahe* to build churches and in all the other lands in his dominions . . .

He shall make his lands free to the Portuguese . . .

Throughout all his kingdom he shall allow as many mines to be sought for and opened as the Portuguese like . . .

Within a year he shall expel all the Moors (i.e. Swahili and Arab traders from the coastal towns) from his kingdom, and those who shall be found there afterward shall be killed by the Portuguese, and their property shall be seized for the king of Portugal.

ACKNOWLEDGMENTS

British Museum (pages 11 bottom, 12 bottom, 17 bottom); Camera Press Ltd (pages 11 top, 13, 14,); David Attenborough (page 20 top); Jos Museum Museum, Nigeria (page 9 top); Mansell Collection (page 12 top); Marc and Evelyne Bernheim from Rapho-Guillumette (page 18); Mary Evans Picture Library (page 15); Paul Popper Ltd (pages 9 bottom, 17 top, 19, 20 bottom); Sudanese Tourist Board (page 6).

Greenhaven World History Program

History Makers
Alexander
Constantine
Leonardo Da Vinci
Columbus
Luther, Erasmus and Loyola
Napoleon
Bolivar
Adam Smith, Malthus and Marx
Darwin
Bismark
Henry Ford
Roosevelt
Stalin
Mao Tse-Tung
Gandhi
Nyerere and Nkrumah

Great Civilizations
The Ancient Near East
Ancient Greece
Pax Romana
The Middle Ages
Spices and Civilization
Chingis Khan and the Mongol Empire
Akbar and the Mughal Empire
Traditional China
Ancient America
Traditional Africa
Asoka and Indian Civilization
Mohammad and the Arab Empire
Ibin Sina and the Muslim World
Suleyman and the Ottoman Empire

Great Revolutions
The Neolithic Revolution
The Agricultural Revolution
The Scientific Revolution
The Industrial Revolution
The Communications Revolution
The American Revolution
The French Revolution
The Mexican Revolution
The Russian Revolution
The Chinese Revolution

Enduring Issues
Cities
Population
Health and Wealth
A World Economy
Law
Religion
Language
Education
The Family

Political and Social Movements
The Slave Trade
The Enlightenment
Imperialism
Nationalism
The British Raj and Indian Nationalism
The Growth of the State
The Suez Canal
The American Frontier
Japan's Modernization
Hitler's Reich
The Two World Wars
The Atom Bomb
The Cold War
The Wealth of Japan
Hollywood